Air Fryer C

GW01158356

What to Cook and How to Get Best Results.

Complete and Effortless Cuisinart Air Fryer Oven Recipes for Beginners.

Affordable Recipes for Smart People on a Budget.

Alexangel Kitchen

Just for Our Readers

To Thank You for Purchasing the Book, for a limited time, you can get a Special FREE BOOK from Alexangel Kitchen

Free Book Here

Or just go to https://alexangelkitchen.com/ **to download your FREE BOOK**

Table of Contents

Introduction

An air fryer uses superheated air in the same way a convection oven works. Differing air frying from a standard oven, as conventional ovens simply heat the air, and convection ovens blow the air around with a fan. Since the air blows around food in a convection cooking is heated more evenly and cooks faster. Since not all kitchens are equipped with a convection oven, the countertop air fryer provides a great alternative. These days, most new full-size and built-in air fryer toaster ovens come with an air fryer function, but here's a sad truth: Most people don't use the air fryer function on their ovens. Why? Because they don't know how to.

Air circulation doesn't just heat the food faster; it also accelerates all the chemical reactions that occur in cooking. The bits of butter in a pastry crust, for example, melt faster, which means they release steam more quickly, which leads to more air between layers—in other words, a flakier crust. When roasting meats, the fat is rendered and the skin is browned more quickly, sealing in juices. The meat, because it cooks more quickly, stays moist, retaining its juicy flavor. The same is true of vegetables—the dry environment created by the fan's air circulation means the sugars caramelize more quickly, locking in moisture and providing deep, round flavor.

Although Air Fryer Toaster Oven cooking seems like new, even though professional chefs have been using it for decades due to its speed and cooking/browning features. Today these ovens are easily available to home cooks at affordable prices.

There are millions of Air Fryer Toaster Oven in private homes today, but people have had to figure out on their own how to adapt their favorite recipes, with varying of success.

How to perfectly use an air fryer toaster oven

Before you use any function to prepare you food, note that you shouldn't use kitchen foil to cover any of the air fryer toast oven accessories as it could stop fat dripping to the pullout tray and an accumulation of fat on the kitchen foil could start a fire.

Air Fry Function

When you think air fry, think of crunchier, healthier and tastier deep frying. The Air Fry function uses cutting edge technology that involves rapid hot air circulation aided by a high-speed fan and upper heating elements to you enjoy fried food without the guilt of consuming too much oil as is the case with deep frying.

When using the Air Fryer Toast Oven, place the basket in the baking pan and place these in the lower rack position. Select Air Fry on the function dial and set the temperature according to your recipe. Turn on the ON/Oven Timer and set to the cooking time that your recipe specifies. The power light will come on and once you're cooking time elapses the ringer will go off once and the oven will automatically shut itself.

Bake Function

For foods that require gentle baking such as cakes, muffins and other pastry, use the bake function. However, if you are looking for extra browning or extra crunch, use convection bake which is ideal for breads, scones, pizza, veggies and roasts.

You can make pizza on the baking pan or you can alternatively buy a pizza stone instead.

Fit your rack and baking pan into the recommended position by your recipe and select bake or convection bake. Set it to ON/ Oven Timer dial to your recipe's time. When baking pastries, you are recommended to preheat your oven for 5 minutes before the actual cook time.

The power light will come on to signify the beginning of cooking. The timer will go off once the cooking time is over and the oven will automatically turn itself off.

Toast Function

Select the toast function and place your food item at the center for even cooking.

Place your rack in the lower position and center the food items. Select toast on your function dial and select Toast/Broil to set your temperature. Turn the ON/ Toast Timer to your level of desired brownness to start toasting.

The power light will come on and once the cycle is over, the ringer will go off once before the oven automatically goes off.

Broil Function

The broil function is perfect for top browning of casseroles, gratins, pies, meats and veggies. You can use the convection broil for meats and fish as it gives a deeper browning.

Gently place the air fryer toast oven basket in the baking pan and either select Broil or Convection Broil. For the temperature, either set it to Broil/ Toast. Next, turn on the ON/ Oven Timer dial to your recipe's specification then start broiling. The power light will come on. Once the cooking is done, the timer will go off once and the oven will automatically turn off.

Note: Do not use glass dishes to broil.

Warm Function

Position the baking pan or oven rack on the lower rack position and set your temperature to warm and choose warm on your function dial. Next set your ON/Oven Timer to the desired time. The power light will come on and the ringer will go off once the time you set elapses. The oven will automatically shut itself.

Spiced Tilapia

Preparation Time: 5 minutes

Cooking Time: 12 minutes

Serving: 2

Ingredients:

- ½ Tsp lemon pepper seasoning
- ½ tsp. Garlic powder
- ½ tsp onion powder
- Salt and ground black pepper, as required
- 2 (6-oz) tilapia fillets
- 1 tbsp olive oil

Directions:

1 In a small bowl, mix together the spices, salt and black pepper. Coat the tilapia fillets with oil and then rub with spice mixture. Arrange the tilapia fillets onto a lightly greased cooking rack, skin-side down.

2 Arrange the drip pan in the bottom of the Instant Vortex Air Fryer Oven cooking chamber. Select "Air Fry" and then adjust the temperature to 360 °F. Set the time for 12 minutes and press "Start".

3　When the display shows "Add Food" insert the cooking rack in the bottom position. When the display shows "Turn Food" turn the fillets.

4　When cooking time is complete, remove the tray from the Vortex Oven. Serve hot.

Nutrition:

Calories 206

Carbs 0.2g

Fat 8.6g

Protein 31.9g

Crispy Tilapia

Preparation Time: 5 minutes

Cooking Time: 15 minutes

Serving: 2

Ingredients:

- ¾ cup cornflakes, crushed
- 1 (1-oz.) packet, dry ranch-style dressing mix
- 2½ tbsp vegetable oil
- 2eggs
- 4 (6-oz) tilapia fillets

Directions:

1. In a shallow bowl, beat the eggs. In another bowl, add the cornflakes, ranch dressing, and oil and mix until a crumbly mixture form. Dip the fish fillets into egg and then, coat with the cornflake mixture.

2. Arrange the tilapia fillets onto the greased cooking tray. Arrange the drip pan in the bottom of the Instant Vortex Air Fryer Oven cooking chamber. Select "Air Fry" and then adjust the temperature to 355 °F. Set the time for 14 minutes and press "Start".

3   When the display shows "Add Food" insert the cooking tray in the center position. When the display shows "Turn Food" turn the tilapia fillets. When cooking time is complete, remove the tray from the Vortex Oven. Serve hot.

Nutrition:

Calories 291

Carbs 4.9g

Fat 14.6g

Protein 34.8g

Crime Chicken

Preparation Time: 5 minutes

Cooking Time: 25 minutes

Serving: 2

Ingredients:

- 2 tbsp. minced garlic
- 1 ½ lbs. boneless skinless chicken thighs
- Pepper and salt as desired
- 1-2 jars of artichokes hearts (10 oz. jars)
- 2 tbsp. oregano

Directions:

1. In a large bowl, mix chicken thighs and artichokes hearts (including liquid) and let it marinate for about 20-30 minutes.
2. After chicken marinates, strain the liquid and toss in remaining spices and garlic. Combine all ingredients.
3. Set broiler on the oven to high and put marinated chicken in for about 18 -25 minutes, so chicken thoroughly cooks.
4. Broil on the second rack for about 18-20 minutes, then broil on the first rack for the last 5 minutes to make chicken a little crispy.

Nutrition:

Calories: 261|

Protein: 33g |

Net Carbs: 5g |

Fat 10

Crispy Haddock

Preparation Time: 5 minutes

Cooking Time: 10 minutes

Serving: 2

Ingredients:

- ½ Cup flour
- ½ tsp. Paprika
- 1 egg, beaten
- ¼ cup mayonnaise
- 4 oz salt and vinegar potato chips, crushed finely
- 1 lb haddock fillet cut into 6 pieces

Direction:

1 In a shallow dish, mix together the flour and paprika. In a second shallow dish, add the egg and mayonnaise and beat well. In a third shallow dish, place the crushed potato chips.

2 Coat the fish pieces with flour mixture, then dip into egg mixture and finally coat with the potato chips. Arrange the fish pieces onto 2 cooking trays.

3   Arrange the drip pan in the bottom of the Instant Vortex Air Fryer Oven cooking chamber. Select "Air Fry" and then adjust the temperature to 370 °F. Set the time for 10 minutes and press "Start".

4   When the display shows "Add Food" insert 1 cooking tray in the top position and another in the bottom position.

5   When the display shows "Turn Food" do not turn the food but switch the position of cooking trays. When cooking time is complete, remove the trays from the Vortex Oven. Serve hot.

Nutrition:

Calories 456

Carbs 40.9g

Fat 22.7g

Protein 43.5g

Vinegar Halibut

Preparation Time: 5 minutes

Cooking Time: 12 minutes

Serving: 2

Ingredients:

- 2 (5-oz) Halibut fillets
- 1 garlic cloves, minced
- 1 tsp fresh rosemary, minced
- 1 tbsp olive oil
- 1 tbsp red wine vinegar
- 1/8 tsp hot sauce

Directions:

1   In a large resealable bag, add all ingredients. Seal the bag and shale well to mix. Refrigerate to marinate for at least 30 minutes Remove the fish fillets from the bag and shake off the excess marinade. Arrange the halibut fillets onto the greased cooking tray.

2   Arrange the drip pan in the bottom of the Instant Vortex Air Fryer Oven cooking chamber. Select "Bake" and then adjust the temperature to 450 °F. Set the time for 12 minutes and press "Start". When the display shows "Add Food" insert the cooking tray in the center position. When the display shows "Turn Food" turn the halibut fillets. When the cooking time is complete, remove the tray from the Vortex Oven. Serve hot.

Nutrition:

Calories 223

Carbs 1g

Fat 10.4g

Protein 30g

Breaded Cod

Preparation Time: 5 minutes

Cooking Time: 10 minutes

Serving: 2

Ingredients:

- 1/3 cup all-purpose flour
- Ground black pepper, as required
- 1 large egg
- 2 tbsp water
- 2/3 cup cornflakes, crushed
- 1 tbsp parmesan cheese, grated
- 1/8 tsp cayenne pepper
- 1 lb. Cod fillets –
- Salt, as required

Directions:

1   In a shallow dish, add the flour and black pepper and mix well. In a second shallow dish, add the egg and water and beat well. In a third shallow dish, add the cornflakes, cheese and cayenne pepper and mix well.

2   Season the cod fillets with salt evenly. Coat the fillets with flour mixture, then dip into egg mixture and finally coat with the cornflake mixture.

3   Arrange the cod fillets onto the greased cooking rack. Arrange the drip pan in the bottom of the Instant Vortex Air Fryer Oven cooking chamber. Select "Air Fry" and then adjust the temperature to 400 °F. Set the time for 10 minutes and press "Start".

4   When the display shows "Add Food" insert the cooking rack in the bottom position. When the display shows "Turn Food" turn the cod fillets. When cooking time is complete, remove the tray from the Vortex Oven. Serve hot.

Nutrition:

Calories 168

Carbs 12.1g

Fat 2.7g

Protein 23.7g

Spicy Catfish

Preparation Time: 5 minutes

Cooking Time: 15 minutes

Serving: 2

Ingredients:

- 2 tbsp cornmeal polenta
- 2 tsp cajun seasoning
- ½ tsp paprika
- ½ tsp garlic powder
- Salt, as required
- 2 (6-oz) catfish fillets
- 1 tbsp olive oil

Directions:

1   In a bowl, mix together the cornmeal, Cajun seasoning, paprika, garlic powder, and salt. Add the catfish fillets and coat evenly with the mixture. Now, coat each fillet with oil.

2   Arrange the fish fillets onto a greased cooking rack and spray with cooking spray. Arrange the drip pan in the bottom of the Instant Vortex Air Fryer Oven cooking chamber. Select "Air Fry" and then adjust the temperature to 400 °F. Set the timer for 14 minutes and press "Start".

3   When the display shows "Add Food" insert the cooking rack in the center position. When the display shows "Turn Food" turn the fillets.

4   When cooking time is complete, remove the rack from the Vortex Oven. Serve hot.

Nutrition:

Calories 32

Carbs 6.7g

Fat 20.3g

Protein 27.3g

Tuna Burgers

Preparation Time: 5 minutes

Cooking Time: 6 minutes

Serving: 2

Ingredients:

- 7 Oz canned tuna
- 1 large egg
- ¼ cup breadcrumbs
- 1 tbsp. Mustard
- ¼ tsp garlic powder
- ¼ tsp onion powder
- ¼ tsp cayenne pepper
- Salt and ground black pepper, as required

Directions:

1 Add all the ingredients into a bowl and mix until well combined. Make 4 equal-sized patties from the mixture.

2 Arrange the patties onto a greased cooking rack. Arrange the drip pan in the bottom of the Instant Vortex Air Fryer Oven cooking chamber. Select "Air Fry" and then adjust the temperature to 400 °F. Set the time for 6 minutes and press "Start".

3   When the display shows "Add Food" insert the cooking rack in the center position.

4   When the display shows "Turn Food" turn the burgers.

5   When the cooking time is complete, remove the tray from the Vortex Oven. Serve hot.

Nutrition:

Calories 151

Carbs 6.3g

Fat 6.4g

Protein 16.4g

Crispy Prawns

Preparation Time: 5 minutes

Cooking Time: 10 minutes

Serving: 2

Ingredients:

- 1egg
- ½ lb crushed nacho chips
- 12prawns, peeled and deveined

Directions:

1 In a shallow dish, beat the egg. In another shallow dish, place the crushed nacho chips. Coat the prawn into egg and then roll into nacho chips.

2 Arrange the coated prawns onto 2 cooking trays in a single layer. Arrange the drip pan in the bottom of the Instant Vortex Air Fryer Oven cooking chamber. Select "Air Fry" and then adjust the temperature to 355 °F. Set the time for 8 minutes and press "Start".

3   When the display shows "Add Food" insert 1
    tray in the top position and another in the
    bottom position. When the display shows "Turn
    Food" do not turn the food but switch the
    position of cooking trays. When cooking time is
    complete, remove the trays from the Vortex
    Oven. Serve hot.

Nutrition:

Calories 386

Carbs 36.1g

Fat 17g

Protein 21g

Prawns in Butter Sauce

Preparation Time: 5 minutes

Cooking Time: 6 minutes

Serving: 2

Ingredients:

- ½ lb. Peeled and deveined large prawns
- 1 large garlic clove, minced
- 1 tbspbutter melted
- 1 tsp fresh lemon zest grated

Directions:

1   Add all the ingredients into a bowl and toss to coat well. Set aside at room temperature for about 30 minutes.

2   Arrange the prawn mixture into a baking dish that will fit in the Vortex Air Fryer Oven. Arrange the drip pan in the bottom of the Instant Vortex Air Fryer Oven cooking chamber. Select "Bake" and then adjust the temperature to 450 °F.

3   Set the time for 6 minutes and press "Start".

4   When the display shows "Add Food" insert the baking dish in the center position. When cooking time is complete, remove the baking dish from the Vortex Oven. When the display shows "Turn Food" do not turn food.

5   When cooking time is complete, remove the baking dish from the Vortex Oven. Serve hot.

Nutrition:

Calories 189

Carbs 2.4g

Fat 7.7g

Protein 26g

Air Fried Chicken Tenderloin

Preparation Time: 5 minutes

Cooking Time: 15 minutes

Serving: 2

Ingredients:

- ½ cup almond flour
- 1 egg, beaten
- 2 tablespoons coconut oil
- 8 chicken tenderloins
- Salt and pepper to taste

Directions:

1   Preheat the air fryer for 5 minutes Season the chicken tenderloin with salt and pepper to taste.

2   Soak in beaten eggs then dredge in almond flour. Place in the air fryer and brush with coconut oil.

3   Cook for 15 minutes at 3750F.

4   Halfway through the cooking time, give the fryer basket a shake to cook evenly.

Nutrition :

Calories 130.3

Carbs 0.7g

Protein 8.7 g

Fat 10.3 g

Almond Flour Battered Chicken Cordon Bleu

Preparation Time: 5 minutes

Cooking Time: 30 minutes

Serving: 2

Ingredients:

- ¼ cup almond flour
- 1 slice cheddar cheese
- 1 slice of ham
- 1 small egg, beaten
- 1 teaspoon parsley
- 2 chicken breasts, butterflied
- Salt and pepper to taste

Directions:

1   Season the chicken with parsley, salt and pepper to taste.
2   Place the cheese and ham in the middle of the chicken and roll. Secure with toothpick.
3   Soak the rolled-up chicken in egg and dredge in almond flour.
4   Place in the air fryer.
5   Cook for 30 minutes at 3500F.

Nutrition :

Calories 1142

Carbs 5.5g

Protein 79.4g

Fat 89.1g

Almond Flour Coco-Milk Battered Chicken

Preparation Time: 5 minutes

Cooking Time: 30 minutes

Serving: 2

Ingredients:

- ¼ cup coconut milk
- ½ cup almond flour
- 1 ½ tablespoons old bay Cajun seasoning
- 1 egg, beaten
- 4 small chicken thighs
- Salt and pepper to taste

Directions:

1 Preheat the air fryer for 5 minutes

2 Mix the egg and coconut milk in a bowl.

3 Soak the chicken thighs in the beaten egg mixture.

4 In a mixing bowl, combine the almond flour, Cajun seasoning, salt and pepper.

5 Dredge the chicken thighs in the almond flour mixture.

6 Place in the air fryer basket.

7 Cook for 30 minutes at 3500F.

Nutrition :

Calories 590

Carbs3.2g

Protein 32.5 g

Fat 38.6g

Bacon 'n Egg-Substitute Bake

Preparation Time: 5 minutes

Cooking Time: 30 minutes

Serving: 2

Ingredients:

- 1 (6 ounce) package Canadian bacon, quartered
- 1/2 cup 2% milk
- 1/4 teaspoon ground mustard
- 1/4 teaspoon salt
- 2 cups shredded Cheddar-Monterey Jack cheese blend
- 3/4 cup and 2 tablespoons egg substitute (such as Egg Beaters® Southwestern Style)
- 4 frozen hash brown patties

Directions:

1 Lightly grease baking pan of air fryer with cooking spray.
2 Evenly spread hash brown patties on bottom of pan. Top evenly with bacon and then followed by cheese.
3 In a bowl, whisk well mustard, salt, milk, and egg substitute. Pour over bacon mixture.
4 Cover air fryer baking pan with foil.
5 Preheat air fryer to 330oF.

6 Cook for another 20 minutes, remove foil and continue cooking for another 15 minutes or until eggs are set.

7 Serve and enjoy.

Nutrition:

Calories 459

Carbs 21.0g

Protein 29.4g

Fat 28.5g

Baked Rice, Black Bean and Cheese

Preparation Time: 5 minutes

Cooking Time: 1 hour

Serving: 2

Ingredients:

- 1 cooked skinless boneless chicken breast halves, chopped
- 1 cup shredded Swiss cheese
- 1/2 (15 ounce) can black beans, Dry out
- 1/2 (4 ounce) can diced green chili peppers, Dry out
- 1/2 cup vegetable broth
- 1/2 medium zucchini, thinly sliced
- 1/4 cup sliced mushrooms
- 1/4 teaspoon cumin
- 1-1/2 teaspoons olive oil
- 2 tablespoons and 2 teaspoons diced onion
- 3 tablespoons brown rice
- 3 tablespoons shredded carrots
- Ground cayenne pepper to taste
- Salt to taste

Directions:

1   Lightly grease baking pan of air fryer with cooking spray. Add rice and broth. Cover pan with foil cook for 10 minutes at 390oF. Lower heat to 300oF and fluff rice. Cook for another 10 minutes Let it stand for 10 minutes and transfer to a bowl and set aside.

2   Add oil to same baking pan. Stir in onion and cook for 5 minutes at 330oF.

3   Stir in mushrooms, chicken, and zucchini. Mix well and cook for 5 minutes

4   Stir in cayenne pepper, salt, and cumin. Mix well and cook for another 2 minutes

5   Stir in ½ of the Swiss cheese, carrots, chilies, beans, and rice. Toss well to mix. Evenly spread in pan. Top with remaining cheese.

6   Cover pan with foil.

7   Cook for 15 minutes at 390oF and then remove foil and cook for another 5 to 10 minutes or until tops are lightly browned.

8   Serve and enjoy.

Nutrition:

Calories 337

Carbs 11.5g

Protein 25.3g

Fat 21.0g

Basil-Garlic Breaded Chicken Bake

Preparation Time: 5 minutes

Cooking Time: 30 minutes

Serving: 2

Ingredients:

- 2 boneless skinless chicken breast halves (4 ounces each)
- 1 tablespoon butter, melted
- 1 large tomato, seeded and chopped
- 2 garlic cloves, minced
- 1 1/2 tablespoons minced fresh basil
- 1/2 tablespoon olive oil
- 1/2 teaspoon salt
- 1/4 cup all-purpose flour
- 1/4 cup egg substitute
- 1/4 cup grated Parmesan cheese
- 1/4 cup dry bread crumbs
- 1/4 teaspoon pepper

Directions:

1   In shallow bowl, whisk well egg substitute and place flour in a separate bowl. Dip chicken in flour, then egg, and then flour. In a small bowl whisk well the butter, bread crumbs and cheese. Sprinkle over chicken.
2   Lightly grease baking pan of air fryer with cooking spray. Place breaded chicken on bottom of pan. Cover with foil.
3   For 20 minutes, cook it on 390 F.
4   Meanwhile, in a bowl whisk well remaining ingredient.
5   Remove foil from pan and then pour over chicken the remaining Ingredients. Cook for 8 minutes. Serve and enjoy.

Nutrition :

Calories 311

Carbs 22.0g

Protein 31.0g

Fat 11.0g

BBQ Chicken Recipe from Greece

Preparation Time: 5 minutes

Cooking Time: 24minutes

Serving: 2

Ingredients:

1   1 (8 ounce) container fat-free plain yogurt
2   2 tablespoons fresh lemon juice
3   2 teaspoons dried oregano
4   1-pound skinless, boneless chicken breast halves - cut into 1-inch pieces
5   1 large red onion, cut into wedges
6   1/2 teaspoon lemon zest
7   1/2 teaspoon salt
8   1 large green bell pepper, cut into 1 1/2-inch pieces
9   1/3 cup crumbled feta cheese with basil and sun-dried tomatoes
10 1/4 teaspoon ground black pepper
11 1/4 teaspoon crushed dried rosemary

Directions:

- In a shallow dish, mix well rosemary, pepper, salt, oregano, lemon juice, lemon zest, feta cheese, and yogurt. Add chicken and toss well to coat. Marinate in the ref for 3 hours.
- Thread bell pepper, onion, and chicken pieces in skewers. Place on skewer rack.
- For 12 minutes, cook it on 360oF. Turnover skewers halfway through cooking time. If needed, cook in batches.
- Serve and enjoy.

Nutrition:

Calories 242

Carbs 12.3g

Protein 31.0g

Fat 7.5g

BBQ Pineapple 'n Teriyaki Glazed Chicken

Preparation Time: 5 minutes

Cooking Time: 20 minutes

Serving: 2

Ingredients:

1   ¼ cup pineapple juice

2   ¼ teaspoon pepper

3   ½ cup brown sugar

4   ½ cup soy sauce

5   ½ teaspoon salt

6   1 green bell pepper, cut into 1-inch cubes

7   1 red bell pepper, cut into 1-inch cubes

8   1 red onion, cut into 1-inch cubes

9   1 Tablespoon cornstarch

10 1 Tablespoon water

11 1 yellow red bell pepper, cut into 1-inch cubes

12 2 boneless skinless chicken breasts cut into 1-inch cubes

13 2 cups fresh pineapple cut into 1-inch cubes

14 2 garlic cloves, minced

15 Green onions, for garnish

Directions:

- In a saucepan, bring to a boil salt, pepper, garlic, pineapple juice, soy sauce, and brown sugar. In a small bowl whisk well, cornstarch and water. Slowly stir in to mixture in pan while whisking constantly. Simmer until thickened, around 3 minutes. Save ¼ cup of the sauce for basting and set aside.
- In shallow dish, mix well chicken and remaining thickened sauce. Toss well to coat. Marinate in the ref for a half hour.
- Thread bell pepper, onion, pineapple, and chicken pieces in skewers. Place on skewer rack in air fryer.
- For 10 minutes, cook on 360oF. Turnover skewers halfway through cooking time. and baste with sauce. If needed, cook in batches.
- Serve and enjoy with a sprinkle of green onions.

Nutrition :

Calories 391

Carbs 58.7g

Protein 31.2g

Fat 3.4g

BBQ Turkey Meatballs with Cranberry Sauce

Preparation Time: 5 minutes

Cooking Time: 20 minutes

Serving: 2

Ingredients:

1   1 ½ tablespoons of water
2   2 teaspoons cider vinegar
3   1 tsp. salt and more to taste
4   1-pound ground turkey
5   1 1/2 tablespoons barbecue sauce
6   1/3 cup cranberry sauce
7   1/4-pound ground bacon

Directions:

- In a bowl, mix well with hands the turkey, ground bacon and a tsp. of salt. Evenly form into 16 equal sized balls.
- In a small saucepan boil cranberry sauce, barbecue sauce, water, cider vinegar, and a dash or two of salt. Mix well and simmer for 3 minutes
- Thread meatballs in skewers and baste with cranberry sauce. Place on skewer rack in air fryer.

- For 15 minutes, cook it on 360oF. Every after 5 minutes of cooking time, turnover skewers and baste with sauce. If needed, cook in batches.
- Serve and enjoy.

Nutrition:

Calories 217

Carbs 11.5g

Protein 28.0g

Fat 10.9g

Blueberry Overload French Toast

Preparation Time: 5 minutes

Cooking Time: 40minutes

Serving: 2

Ingredients:

1. 1 (8 ounce) package cream cheese, cut into 1-inch cubes
2. 1 cup fresh blueberries, divided
3. 1 cup milk
4. 1 tablespoon cornstarch
5. 1/2 cup water
6. 1/2 cup white sugar
7. 1/2 teaspoon vanilla extract
8. 1-1/2 teaspoons butter
9. 2 tablespoons and 2 teaspoons maple syrup
10. 6 eggs, beaten
11. 6 slices day-old bread, cut into 1-inch cubes

Directions:

- Lightly grease baking pan of air fryer with cooking spray.
- Evenly spread half of the bread on bottom of pan. Sprinkle evenly the cream cheese and ½ cup blueberries. Add remaining bread on top.

- In a large bowl, whisk well eggs, milk, syrup, and vanilla extract. Pour over bread mixture.
- Cover air fryer baking pan with foil and refrigerate overnight.
- Preheat air fryer to 330oF.
- Cook for 25 minutes covered in foil, remove foil and cook for another 20 minutes or until middle is set.
- Meanwhile, make the sauce by mixing cornstarch, water, and sugar in a saucepan and bring to a boil. Stir in remaining blueberries and simmer until thickened and blueberries have burst.
- Serve and enjoy with blueberry syrup.

Nutrition :

Calories 492

Carbs 51.9g

Protein 15.1g

Fat 24.8g

Broccoli-Rice 'n Cheese Casserole

Preparation Time: 5 minutes

Cooking Time: 30 minutes

Serving: 2

Ingredients:

1. 1 (10 ounce) can chunk chicken, Dry out
2. 1 cup uncooked instant rice
3. 1 cup water
4. 1/2 (10.75 ounce) can condensed cream of chicken soup
5. 1/2 (10.75 ounce) can condensed cream of mushroom soup
6. 1/2 cup milk
7. 1/2 small white onion, chopped
8. 1/2-pound processed cheese food
9. 2 tablespoons butter
10. 8-ounce frozen chopped broccoli

Directions:

- Lightly grease baking pan of air fryer with cooking spray. Add water and bring to a boil at 390oF. Stir in rice and cook for 3 minutes.

- Stir in processed cheese, onion, broccoli, milk, butter, chicken soup, mushroom soup, and chicken. Mix well. Cook for 15 minutes at 390oF, fluff mixture and continue cooking for another 10 minutes until tops are browned. Serve and enjoy.

Nutrition:

Calories 752

Carbs 82.7g

Protein 36.0g

Fat 30.8g

Buffalo Style Chicken Dip

Preparation Time: 5 minutes

Cooking Time: 10 minutes

Serving: 2

Ingredients:

1 1 (8 ounce) package cream cheese, softened

2 1 tablespoon shredded pepper Jack cheese

3 1/2 pinch cayenne pepper, for garnish

4 1/2 pinch cayenne pepper, or to taste

5 1/4 cup and 2 tablespoons hot pepper sauce (such as Frank's Reshoot®)

6 1/4 cup blue cheese dressing

7 1/4 cup crumbled blue cheese

8 1/4 cup shredded pepper Jack cheese

9 1/4 teaspoon seafood seasoning (such as Old Bay®)

10 1-1/2 cups diced cooked rotisserie chicken

Directions:

- Lightly grease baking pan of air fryer with cooking spray. Mix in cayenne pepper, seafood seasoning, crumbled blue cheese, blue cheese dressing, pepper Jack, hot pepper sauce, cream cheese, and chicken.
- For 15 minutes, cook it on 390 F.

- Let it stand for 5 minutes and garnish with cayenne pepper.
- Serve and enjoy.

Nutrition:

Calories 405

Carbs 3.2g

Protein 17.1g

Fat 35.9g

Buttered Spinach-Egg Omelet

Preparation Time: 5 minutes

Cooking Time: 10 minutes

Serving: 2

Ingredients:

1. ¼ cup coconut milk
2. 1 tablespoon melted butter
3. 1-pound baby spinach, chopped finely
4. 3 tablespoons olive oil
5. 4 eggs, beaten
6. Salt and pepper to taste

Directions:

- Preheat the air fryer for 5 minutes. In a mixing bowl, combine the eggs, coconut milk, olive oil, and butter until well-combined.
- Add the spinach and season with salt and pepper to taste. Pour all ingredients in a baking dish that will fit in the air fryer. Bake at 3500F for 15 minutes

Nutrition:

Calories 310

Carbs 3.6g

Protein 13.6g

Fat 26.8g

Caesar Marinated Grilled Chicken

Preparation Time: 5 minutes

Cooking Time: 20 minutes

Serving: 2

Ingredients:

1   ¼ cup crouton
2   1 teaspoon lemon zest. Form into ovals, skewer and grill.
3   1/2 cup Parmesan
4   1/4 cup breadcrumbs
5   1-pound ground chicken
6   2 tablespoons Caesar dressing and more for drizzling
7   2-4 romaine leaves

Directions:

- In a shallow dish, mix well chicken, 2 tablespoons Caesar dressing, parmesan, and breadcrumbs. Mix well with hands. Form into 1-inch oval patties.
- Thread chicken pieces in skewers. Place on skewer rack in air fryer.

- For 12 minutes, cook it on 360oF. Turnover skewers halfway through cooking time. If needed, cook in batches.
- Serve and enjoy on a bed of lettuce and sprinkle with croutons and extra dressing.

Nutrition :

Calories 339

Carbs 9.5g

Protein 32.6g

Fat 18.9g

Cheese Stuffed Chicken

Preparation Time: 5 minutes

Cooking Time: 25 minutes

Serving: 2

Ingredients:

1. 1 tablespoon creole seasoning
2. 1 tablespoon olive oil
3. 1 teaspoon garlic powder
4. 1 teaspoon onion powder
5. 4 chicken breasts, butterflied and pounded
6. 4 slices Colby cheese
7. 4 slices pepper jack cheese

Directions:

- Preheat the air fryer to 3900F.
- Place the grill pan accessory in the air fryer.
- Create the dry rub by mixing in a bowl the creole seasoning, garlic powder, and onion powder. Season it with salt and pepper if desired.
- Rub the seasoning on to the chicken.
- Place the chicken on a working surface and place a slice each of pepper jack and Colby cheese.

- Fold the chicken and secure the edges with toothpicks.
- Brush chicken with olive oil.
- Grill for 30 minutes and make sure to flip the meat every 10 minutes

Nutrition :

Calories 727

Carbs 5.4 g

Protein 73.1g

Fat 45.9g

Cheeseburger Egg Rolls

Preparation Time: 10 minutes

Cooking Time: 7 minutes

Servings: 2

Ingredients:

1   6 egg roll wrappers

2   6 chopped dill pickle chips

3   1 tbsp. yellow mustard

4   3 tbsp. cream cheese

5   3 tbsp. shredded cheddar cheese

6   ½ C. chopped onion

7   ½ C. chopped bell pepper

8   ¼ tsp. onion powder

9   ¼ tsp. garlic powder

10 8 ounces of raw lean ground beef

Directions:

- In a skillet, add seasonings, beef, onion, and bell pepper. Stir and crumble beef till fully cooked, and vegetables are soft.

- Take skillet off the heat and add cream cheese, mustard, and cheddar cheese, stirring till melted.

- Pour beef mixture into a bowl and fold in pickles.

- Lay out egg wrappers and place 1/6th of beef mixture into each one. Moisten egg roll wrapper edges with water. Fold sides to the middle and seal with water.
- Repeat with all other egg rolls.
- Place rolls into air fryer, one batch at a time.
- Pour into the Oven rack/basket. Place the Rack on the middle-shelf of the Air Fryer Oven. Set temperature to 392°F, and set time to 7 minutes

Nutrition:

Calories 153 Cal

Fat 4 g

Carbs 0 g

Protein 12 g

Air Fried Grilled Steak

Preparation Time: 5 minutes

Cooking Time: 45 minutes

Servings: 2

Ingredients:

1   2 top sirloin steaks

2   3 tablespoons butter, melted

3   3 tablespoons olive oil

4   Salt and pepper to taste

Directions:

- Preheat the Air Fryer Oven for 5 minutes. Season the sirloin steaks with olive oil, salt and pepper.
- Place the beef in the air fryer basket.
- Cook for 45 minutes at 350°F.
- Once cooked, serve with butter.

Nutrition:

Calories 1536

Fat 123.7 g

Carbs 0 g

Protein 103.4 g

Juicy Cheeseburgers

Preparation Time: 5 minutes

Cooking Time: 15 minutes

Servings: 2

Ingredients:

1   1 pound 93% lean ground beef

2   1 teaspoon Worcestershire sauce

3   1 tablespoon burger seasoning

4   Salt

5   Pepper

6   Cooking oil

7   4 slices cheese

8   Buns

Directions:

- In a large bowl, mix the ground beef, Worcestershire, burger seasoning, and salt and pepper to taste until well blended. Spray the air fryer basket with cooking oil. You will need only a quick sprits. The burgers will produce oil as they cook. Shape the mixture into 4 patties. Place the burgers in the air fryer. The burgers should fit without the need to stack, but stacking is okay if necessary.

- Pour into the Oven rack/basket. Place the Rack on the middle-shelf of the Air Fryer Oven. Set temperature to 375°F, and set time to 8 minutes Cook for 8 minutes Open the air fryer and flip the burgers. Cook for an additional 3 to 4 minutes Check the inside of the burgers to determine if they have finished cooking. You can stick a knife or fork in the center to examine the color.
- Top each burger with a slice of cheese. Cook for an additional minute, or until the cheese has melted
- Serve on buns with any additional toppings of your choice.

Nutrition:

Calories 566 Cal

Fat 39 g

Carbs 0 g

Protein 29 g

Spicy Thai Beef Stir-Fry

Preparation Time: 15 minutes

Cooking Time: 9 minutes

Servings: 2

Ingredients:

- 1-pound sirloin steaks, thinly sliced
- 2 tablespoons lime juice, divided
- ⅓Cup crunchy peanut butter
- ½ cup beef broth
- 1 tablespoon olive oil
- 1½ cups broccoli florets
- 2 cloves garlic, sliced
- 1 to 2 red chili peppers, sliced

Directions:

1 In a medium bowl, combine the steak with 1 tablespoon of the lime juice. Set aside.

2 Combine the peanut butter and beef broth in a small bowl and mix well. Dry out the beef and add the juice from the bowl into the peanut butter mixture.

3 In a 6-inch metal bowl, combine the olive oil, steak, and broccoli.

4   Pour into the Oven rack/basket. Place the Rack on the middle-shelf of the Air Fryer Oven. Set temperature to 375°F, and set time to 4 minutes Cook for 3 to 4 minutes or until the steak is almost cooked and the broccoli is crisp and tender, shaking the basket once during cooking time.

5   Add the garlic, chili peppers, and the peanut butter mixture and stir.

6   Cook for 3 to 5 minutes or until the sauce is bubbling and the broccoli is tender.

7   Serve over hot rice.

Nutrition:

Calories 387 Cal

Fat 22 g

Carbs 0 g

Protein 42 g

Beef Brisket Recipe from Texas

Preparation Time: 15 minutes

Cooking Time: 1 hour and 30 minutes

Servings: 2

Ingredients:

- 1 ½ cup beef stock
- 1 bay leaf
- 1 tablespoon garlic powder
- 1 tablespoon onion powder
- 2 pounds beef brisket, trimmed
- 2 tablespoons chili powder
- 2 teaspoons dry mustard
- 4 tablespoons olive oil
- Salt and pepper to taste

Directions:

1. Preheat the Air Fryer Oven for 5 minutes Place all ingredients in a deep baking dish that will fit in the air fryer.
2. Bake it for 1 hour and 30 minutes at 400°F.
3. Stir the beef every after 30 minutes to soak in the sauce.

Nutrition:

Calories 306 Cal

Fat 24.1 g

Carbs 0 g

Protein 18.3 g

Copycat Taco Bell Crunch Wraps

Preparation Time: 10 minutes

Cooking Time: 2 minutes

Servings: 2

Ingredients:

- 6 wheat tostadas
- 2 C. sour cream
- 2 C. Mexican blend cheese
- 2 C. shredded lettuce
- 12 ounces low-sodium nacho cheese
- 3 Roma tomatoes
- 6 12-inch wheat tortillas
- 1 1/3 C. water
- 2 packets low-sodium taco seasoning
- 2 pounds of lean ground beef

Directions:

1   Ensure your air fryer is preheated to 400 degrees.

2   Make beef according to taco seasoning packets.

3   Place 2/3 C. prepared beef, 4 tbsp. cheese, 1 tostada, 1/3 C. sour cream, 1/3 C. lettuce, 1/6th of tomatoes and 1/3 C. cheese on each tortilla.

4   Fold up tortillas edges and repeat with remaining ingredients.

5   Lay the folded sides of tortillas down into the air fryer and spray with olive oil.

6   Set temperature to 400°F, and set time to 2 minutes Cook 2 minutes till browned.

Nutrition:

Calories 311 Cal

Fat 9 g

Carbs 0 g

Protein 22 g

Air Fryer Beef Casserole

Preparation Time: 5 minutes

Cooking Time: 30 minutes

Servings: 2

Ingredients:

- 1 green bell pepper, seeded and chopped
- 1 onion, chopped
- 1-pound ground beef
- 3 cloves of garlic, minced
- 3 tablespoons olive oil
- 6 cups eggs, beaten
- Salt and pepper to taste

Directions:

1   Preheat the Air Fryer Oven for 5 minutes
2   In a baking dish that will fit in the air fryer, mix the ground beef, onion, garlic, olive oil, and bell pepper. Season it with salt and pepper to taste.
3   Pour in the beaten eggs and give a good stir.
4   Place the dish with the beef and egg mixture in the air fryer.
5   Pour into the Oven rack/basket. Place the Rack on the middle-shelf of the Air Fryer Oven. Set temperature to 325°F, and set time to 30 minutes. Bake it for 30 minutes

Nutrition:

Calories 1520 Cal

Fat 125.11 g

Carbs 0 g

Protein 87.9 g

Meat Lovers' Pizza

Preparation Time: 10 minutes

Cooking Time: 12 minutes

Servings: 2

Ingredients:

- 1 pre-prepared 7-inch pizza pie crust, defrosted if necessary
- 1/3 cup of marinara sauce
- 2 ounces of grilled steak, sliced into bite-sized pieces
- 2 ounces of salami, sliced fine
- 2 ounces of pepperoni, sliced fine
- ¼ cup of American cheese
- ¼ cup of shredded mozzarella cheese

Directions:

1 Preheat the Air Fryer Oven to 350 degrees. Lay the pizza dough flat on a sheet of parchment paper or tin foil, cut large enough to hold the entire pie crust, but small enough that it will leave the edges of the air frying basket uncovered to allow for air circulation.

2   Using a fork, stab the pizza dough several times across the surface – piercing the pie crust will allow air to circulate throughout the crust and ensure even cooking. With a deep soup spoon, ladle the marinara sauce onto the pizza dough, and spread evenly in expanding circles over the surface of the pie-crust. Be sure to leave at least ½ inch of bare dough around the edges, to ensure that extra-crispy crunchy first bite of the crust! Distribute the pieces of steak and the slices of salami and pepperoni evenly over the sauce-covered dough, then sprinkle the cheese in an even layer on top.

3   Set the air fryer timer to 12 minutes, and place the pizza with foil or paper on the fryer's basket surface. Again, be sure to leave the edges of the basket uncovered to allow for proper air circulation, and don't let your bare fingers touch the hot surface. After 12 minutes, when the Air Fryer Oven shuts off, the cheese should be perfectly melted and lightly crisped, and the pie crust should be golden brown. Using a spatula – or two, if necessary, remove the pizza from the air fryer basket and set on a serving plate. Wait a few minutes until the pie is cool enough to handle, then cut into slices and serve.

Nutrition:

Calories 390 Cal

Fat 21 g

Carbs 34 g

Fiber 3 g

Chimichurri Skirt Steak

Preparation Time: 10 minutes

Cooking Time: 8 minutes

Servings: 2

Ingredients:

- 2 x 8 oz. skirt steak
- 1 cup finely chopped parsley
- ¼ cup finely chopped mint
- 2 tbsp. fresh oregano (washed & finely chopped)
- 3 finely chopped cloves of garlic
- 1 tsp. red pepper flakes (crushed)
- 1 tbsp. ground cumin
- 1 tsp. cayenne pepper
- 2 tsp. smoked paprika
- 1 tsp. salt
- ¼ tsp. pepper
- ¾ cup oil
- 3 tbsp. red wine vinegar

Directions:

1. Throw all the ingredients in a bowl (besides the steak) and mix well.

2   Put ¼ cup of the mixture in a plastic baggie with the steak and leave in the fridge overnight (2–24hrs).

3   Leave the bag out at room temperature for at least 30 min before popping into the air fryer. Preheat for a minute or two to 390° F before cooking until med–rare (8–10 min). Pour into the Oven rack/basket. Place the Rack on the middle-shelf of the Air Fryer Oven. Set temperature to 390°F, and set time to 10 minutes

4   Put 2 Tbsp. of the chimichurri mix on top of each steak before serving.

Nutrition:

Calories 308.6 Cal

Fat 22.6 g

Carbs 3 g

Protein 23.7 g

Country Fried Steak

Preparation Time: 5 minutes

Cooking Time: 12 minutes

Servings: 2

Ingredients:

- 1 tsp. pepper
- 2 C. almond milk
- 2 tbsp. almond flour
- 6 ounces ground sausage meat
- 1 tsp. pepper
- 1 tsp. salt
- 1 tsp. garlic powder
- 1 tsp. onion powder
- 1 C. panko breadcrumbs
- 1 C. almond flour
- 3 beaten eggs
- 6 ounces sirloin steak, pounded till thin

Directions:

1. Season panko breadcrumbs with spices
2. Dredge steak in flour, then egg, and then seasoned panko mixture.
3. Place into air fryer basket.
4. Set temperature to 370°F, and set time to 12 minutes

5   To make sausage gravy, cook sausage and Dry out of fat, but reserve 2 tablespoons.

6   Add flour to sausage and mix until incorporated. Gradually mix in milk over medium to high heat till it becomes thick.

7   Season mixture with pepper and cook 3 minutes longer.

8   Serve steak topped with gravy and enjoy.

Nutrition:

Calories 395 Cal

Fat 11 g

Carbs 0 g

Protein 39 g

Creamy Burger & Potato Bake

Preparation Time: 5 minutes

Cooking Time: 55 minutes

Servings: 2

Ingredients:

- Salt to taste
- Freshly ground pepper, to taste
- 1/2 (10.75 ounce) can condensed cream of mushroom soup
- 1/2-pound lean ground beef
- 1-1/2 cups peeled and thinly sliced potatoes
- 1/2 cup shredded Cheddar cheese
- 1/4 cup chopped onion
- 1/4 cup and 2 tablespoons milk

Directions:

1 Lightly grease baking pan of air fryer with cooking spray. Add ground beef. For 10 minutes, cook on 360°F
2 Stir and crumble halfway through cooking time.
3 Meanwhile, in a bowl, whisk well pepper, salt, milk, onion, and mushroom soup. Mix well.
4 Dry out fat off ground beef and transfer beef to a plate.

5   In same air fryer baking pan, layer ½ of potatoes on bottom, then ½ of soup mixture, and then ½ of beef. Repeat process.

6   Cover pan with foil.

7   Cook for 30 minutes Remove foil and cook for another 15 minutes or until potatoes are tender.

8   Serve and enjoy.

Nutrition:

Calories 399 Cal

Fat 26.9 g

Carbs 0 g

Protein 22.1 g

Beefy 'n Cheesy Spanish Rice Casserole

Preparation Time: 10 minutes

Cooking Time: 50 minutes

Servings: 2

Ingredients:

- 2 tablespoons chopped green bell pepper
- 1 tablespoon chopped fresh cilantro
- 1/2-pound lean ground beef
- 1/2 cup water
- 1/2 teaspoon salt
- 1/2 teaspoon brown sugar
- 1/2 pinch ground black pepper
- 1/3 cup uncooked long grain rice
- 1/4 cup finely chopped onion
- 1/4 cup chili sauce
- 1/4 teaspoon ground cumin
- 1/4 teaspoon Worcestershire sauce
- 1/4 cup shredded Cheddar cheese
- 1/2 (14.5 ounce) can canned tomatoes

Directions:

- Lightly grease baking pan of air fryer with cooking spray. Add ground beef.

- For 10 minutes, cook on 360°F Halfway through cooking time, stir and crumble beef. Discard excess fat,
- Stir in pepper, Worcestershire sauce, cumin, brown sugar, salt, chili sauce, rice, water, tomatoes, green bell pepper, and onion. Mix well. Cover pan with foil and cook for 25 minutes. Stirring occasionally
- Give it one last good stir, press down firmly and sprinkle cheese on top.
- Cook uncovered for 15 minutes at 390°F until tops are lightly browned.
- Serve and enjoy with chopped cilantro.

Nutrition:

Calories 346 Cal

Fat 19.1 g

Carbs 0 g

Protein 18.5 g

Warming Winter Beef with Celery

Preparation Time: 5 minutes

Cooking Time: 12 minutes

Servings: 2

Ingredients:

1. 9 ounces tender beef, chopped
2. 1/2 cup leeks, chopped
3. 1/2 cup celery stalks, chopped
4. 2 cloves garlic, smashed
5. 2 tablespoons red cooking wine
6. 3/4 cup cream of celery soup
7. 2 sprigs rosemary, chopped
8. 1/4 teaspoon smoked paprika
9. 3/4 teaspoons salt
10. 1/4 teaspoon black pepper, or to taste

Directions:

- Add the beef, leeks, celery, and garlic to the baking dish; cook for about 5 minutes at 390 degrees F.
- Once the meat is starting to tender, pour in the wine and soup. Season with rosemary, smoked paprika, salt, and black pepper
- Now, cook an additional 7 minutes

Nutrition:

Calories 364 Cal

Fat 9 g

Carbs 39 g

Protein 32 g

Beef & veggie Spring Rolls

Preparation Time: 5 minutes

Cooking Time: 12 minutes

Servings: 2

Ingredients:

1   2-ounce Asian rice noodles
2   1 tablespoon sesame oil
3   7-ounce ground beef
4   1 small onion, chopped
5   3 garlic cloves, crushed
6   1 cup fresh mixed vegetables
7   1 teaspoon soy sauce
8   1 packet spring roll skins
9   2 tablespoons water
10 Olive oil, as required

Directions:

- Soak the noodles in warm water till soft.
- Dry out and cut into small lengths. In a pan heat the oil and add the onion and garlic and sauté for about 4-5 minutes
- Add beef and cook for about 4-5 minutes
- Add vegetables and cook for about 5-7 minutes or till cooked through.
- Stir in soy sauce and remove from the heat.

- Immediately, stir in the noodles and keep aside till all the juices have been absorbed.
- Preheat the Air Fryer Oven to 350 degrees F.
- Place the spring rolls skin onto a smooth surface.
- Add a line of the filling diagonally across.
- Fold the top point over the filling and then fold in both sides.
- On the final point, brush it with water before rolling to seal.
- Brush the spring rolls with oil.
- Arrange the rolls in batches in the air fryer and Cook for about 8 minutes
- Repeat with remaining rolls. Now, place spring rolls onto a baking sheet.
- Bake it for about 6 minutes per side.

Nutrition:

Calories 364 Cal

Fat 9 g

Carbs 39 g

Protein 32 g

Charred Onions and Steak Cube BBQ

Preparation Time: 5 minutes
Cooking Time: 40 minutes
Servings: 2
Ingredients:

- 1 cup red onions cut into wedges
- 1 tablespoon dry mustard
- 1 tablespoon olive oil
- 1-pound boneless beef sirloin, cut into cubes
- Salt and pepper to taste

Directions:

- Preheat the air fryer to 390°F.
- Place the grill pan accessory in the air fryer.
- Toss all ingredients in a bowl and mix until everything is coated with the seasonings.
- Place on the grill pan and cook for 40 minutes
- Halfway through the cooking time, give a stir to cook evenly.

Nutrition:

Calories 260 Cal

Fat 10.7 g

Carbs 0 g

Protein 35.5 g

Easy Air Fried Roasted Asparagus

Preparation Time: 5 minutes

Cooking Time: 10 minutes

Servings: 2

Ingredients:

- 1 bunch fresh asparagus
- 1 ½ tsp. herbs de provence
- Fresh lemon wedge (optional)
- 1 tablespoon olive oil or cooking spray
- Salt and pepper to taste

Directions:

1   Wash asparagus and trim off hard ends. Drizzle with asparagus with olive oil and add seasonings

2   Place asparagus in air fryer and cook on 360F for 6 to 10 minutes

3   Drizzle with squeezed lemon over roasted asparagus.

Nutrition:

Calories 46

Protein 2g

Fat 3g

Carbs 1g

Air Fryer Roasted Broccoli

Preparation Time: 5 minutes

Cooking Time: 10 minutes

Servings: 2

Ingredients:

- 1 tsp. herbes de provence seasoning (optional)
- 4 cups fresh broccoli
- 1 tablespoon olive oil
- Salt and pepper to taste

Directions:

1. Drizzle with or spray broccoli with olive and sprinkle seasoning throughout
2. Spray air fryer basket with cooking oil, place broccoli and cook for 5-8 minutes on 360F
3. Open air fryer and examine broccoli after 5 minutes because different fryer brands cook at different rates.

Nutrition:

Calories 61

Fat 4g

Protein 3g

Carbs 4g

Air Fryer Veggie Quesadillas

Preparation Time: 20 minutes

Cooking Time: 20 minutes

Servings: 2

Ingredients:

- 4 sprouted whole-grain flour tortillas (6-in.)
- 1 cup sliced red bell pepper
- 4 ounces reduced-fat Cheddar cheese, shredded
- 1 cup sliced zucchini
- 1 cup canned black beans, dry out and rinsed (no salt)
- Cooking spray
- 2 ounces plain 2% reduced-fat Greek yogurt
- 1 teaspoon lime zest
- 1 Tbsp. fresh juice (from 1 lime)
- ¼ tsp. ground cumin
- 2 tablespoons chopped fresh cilantro
- 1/2 cup Dry out refrigerated pico de gallo

Directions:

1   Place tortillas on work surface, sprinkle 2 tablespoons shredded cheese over half of each tortilla and top with cheese on each tortilla with 1/4 cup each red pepper slices, zucchini slices, and black beans. Sprinkle evenly with remaining 1/2 cup cheese.

2   Fold tortillas over to form half-moon shaped quesadillas, lightly coat with cooking spray, and secure with toothpicks.

3   Lightly spray air fryer basket with cooking spray. Place 2 quesadillas in the basket, and cook at 400°F for 10 minutes until tortillas are golden brown and slightly crispy, cheese is melted, and vegetables are slightly softened. Turn quesadillas over halfway through cooking.

4   Repeat with remaining quesadillas. Meanwhile, stir yogurt, lime juice, lime zest and cumin in a small bowl. Cut each quesadilla into wedges and sprinkle with cilantro.

5   Serve with 1 tablespoon cumin cream and 2 tablespoons pico de gallo each.

Nutrition:

Calories 291

Fat 8g

Protein 17g

Carbs 36g

Air Fryer Buffalo Mushroom Poppers

Preparation Time: 30 minutes

Cooking Time: 50 minutes

Servings: 2

Ingredients:

- 1-pound fresh whole button mushrooms
- 1/2 teaspoon kosher salt
- 3 tablespoons 1/3-less-fat cream cheese,
- 1/4 cup all-purpose flour
- Softened 1 jalapeño chili, seeded and minced

Cooking spray

1   1/4 teaspoon black pepper

2   1 cup panko breadcrumbs

3   2 large eggs, lightly beaten

4   1/4 cup buffalo-style hot sauce

5   2 tablespoons chopped fresh chives

6   1/2 cup low-fat buttermilk

7   1/2 cup plain fat-free yogurt

8   2 ounces blue cheese, crumbled (about 1/2 cup)

9   3 tablespoons apple cider vinegar

Directions:

- Remove stems from mushroom caps, chop stems and set caps aside. Stir together chopped mushroom stems, cream cheese, jalapeño, salt, and pepper. Stuff about 1 teaspoon of the mixture into each mushroom cap, rounding the filling to form a smooth ball.
- Place panko in a bowl, place flour in a second bowl, and eggs in a third Coat mushrooms in flour, dip in egg mixture, and dredge in panko, pressing to adhere. Spray mushrooms well with cooking spray.
- Place half of the mushrooms in air fryer basket, and cook for 20 minutes at 350°F. Transfer cooked mushrooms to a large bowl. Drizzle with buffalo sauce over mushrooms; toss to coat then sprinkle with chives.
- Stir buttermilk, yogurt, blue cheese, and cider vinegar in a small bowl. Serve mushroom poppers with blue cheese sauce.

Nutrition:

Calories 133

Fat 4g

Protein 7g

Carbs 16g

Crispy Cheesy Vegan Quesarito

Preparation Time: 5 minutes

Cooking Time: 10 minutes

Servings: 2

Ingredients:

1   2 large gluten free tortillas

2   4 tablespoons Vegan Queso (divided)

3   2-3 tablespoons grated cheese

4   3 tablespoons Meaty Crumbles

5   3-4 tablespoons Simple Spanish rice

6   1-2 tablespoons Spicy Almond Sauce

7   1 tablespoon cashew cream or dairy free sour cream

Added ingredients

- Fresh baby spinach, Fresh bell peppers
- Roasted red peppers

Directions:

- Lay first tortilla flat on prep surface.
- Cut about an inch from around the entire edge of the second tortilla using a knife, making one smaller tortilla and then set aside.
- On the first tortilla, spread the vegan queso around the middle of the tortilla, in a circle the size of the smaller tortilla.

- Add 3 tablespoons grated cheese to the top of the queso, in an even layer across the small circle (1 tablespoon grated cheese)
- Top the queso / cheese circle with the smaller second tortilla, and press down slightly.
- Spoon a line of the meaty crumbles onto the middle of the second smaller tortilla, spoon the Spanish rice on top of the meaty crumbles, followed by the tangy cream sauce and cashew cream / sour cream.
- Carefully fold and roll burrito tightly. Secure the edge with the reserved 1 tablespoon grated cheese. Place the burrito cheese sealed side down in air fryer basket.
- Fry for 6-7 minutes at 370°F, or until lightly golden and crisp.

Nutrition:

Calories 514

Fat 18g

Carbs 13g

Protein 22g

Roasted Heirloom Tomato with Baked Feta

Preparation Time: 20 minutes

Cooking Time: 14 minutes

Servings: 2

Ingredients:

1. 1 ea. Heirloom tomato
2. 8 oz. Feta cheese block
3. ½ cup red onions (sliced paper thin)
4. 1 tbsp. Olive oil

For Basil Pesto:

1. ½ cup parsley (rough chopped)
2. ½ cup basil (rough chopped)
3. ½ cup parmesan (freshly grated)
4. 3 tbsp toasted pine nuts
5. 1 ea. Garlic clove
6. ½ cup olive oil
7. 1 pinch salt

Directions:

- Preheat the Air fryer to 390°F.
- Combine pine nuts, 1 tsp. olive oil, and pinch of salt.

- Toss pine nuts into the Air fryer and set timer for 2 minutes Remove and place onto a paper towel and set aside.
- Wash and chop one bunch of parsley and one bunch of basil.
- Place chopped parsley, basil, fresh grated parmesan, garlic, toasted pine nuts and salt in a small pot over medium-high heat.
- Turn on the food processor and Drizzle with in the olive oil.
- Remove the pesto and refrigerate.
- Slice the tomato into ½ inch thick slices. Slice the feta into ½ inch thick slices. Take a circle cutter and cut the feta the same size as the heirloom tomato.
- Stack the feta on top of the tomato, spread 1 tablespoon basil pesto in between.
- Slice the red onions paper thin and toss with 1 tablespoon of olive oil and apply to the top of the feta.
- Place tomatoes into the Air fryer and cook for 12-14 minutes
- Finish with sea salt and basil pesto.

Nutrition:

Calories 322.2

Fat 30.8g

Carbs 7.7.G

Protein 32g

Cheese and Veggie Cups

Preparation Time: 10 minutes

Cooking Time: 20 minutes

Servings: 2

Ingredients:

1   Non-stick cooking spray

2   4 large eggs

3   1 cup diced veggies of choice

4   1 cup shredded cheese

5   4 Tbsp. half and half

6   1 Tbsp. chopped cilantro

7   Salt and Pepper

Directions:

- Grease 4 ramekins
- Whisk eggs, vegetables, half the cheese, half and half, cilantro, and salt and pepper together. In a medium bowl and divide between the ramekins
- Place ramekins in the air-fryer basket, set temperature to 300 F for 12 minutes
- Top the cups with remaining cheese.
- Set air-fryer to 400 degrees F, cook 2 minutes until cheese is melted.

Nutrition:

Calories 195kcal

Carbs 7g

Protein 13g

Fat 12g

Air Fryer Vegetables

Preparation Time: 5 minutes

Cooking Time: 10 minutes

Servings: 2

Ingredients:

1. 1/2 lb. broccoli fresh
2. 1/2 lb. cauliflower fresh
3. 1 tbsp. Olive oil
4. 1/4 tsp. seasoning
5. 1/3 c water

Directions:

- Mix vegetables, olive oil and seasonings in a medium bowl.
- Pour 1/3 c. water in the Air Fryer base to prevent from smoking.
- Place vegetables in the air fryer basket.
- Cook at 400 degrees for 7-10 minutes
- Shake vegetables half way through the 7-10 minutes

Nutrition:

Calories 65kcal

Carbs 7g

Protein 3g

Fat 4g

Mushroom, Onion and Feta Frittata

Preparation Time: 15 minutes

Cooking Time: 10 minutes

Servings: 2

Ingredients:

1. 3 whole eggs
2. 2 cup sliced button mushrooms
3. ½ red onions
4. 1 tbsp. Olive oil
5. 3 tbsp crumbled feta
6. 1 pinch salt

Directions:

- Peel and slice half a red onion into ¼ inch thin slices.
- Wash button mushrooms; then slice into ¼ inch thin slices.
- Place a pan under a medium flame, add olive oil sweat onions and mushrooms and sauté until tender.Take onions and mushrooms off the heat and place on kitchen towel to cool.
- Preheat Air fryer to 320°F.
- In a mixing bowl crack 3 eggs and whisk thoroughly and vigorously.

- Coat the outside and bottom of a 6-ounce ramekin lightly with pan spray.
- Pour eggs into the ramekin, add ¼ cup onion and mushrooms mixture, and then add cheese.
- Place in Air fryer and cook for 10 to 12 minutes

Nutrition:

Calories 90

Fat 4.5g

Carbs 8g

Protein 13g

Sweet and Spicy Air Fryer Brussels Sprouts

Preparation Time: 5 minutes

Cooking Time: 20 minutes

Servings: 2

Ingredients:

1   1 Brussels sprout cut into two halves

2   1 ½ tablespoon vegetable oil

3   ½ tsp. salt

4   2 tablespoon honey

5   1 tablespoon gochujang

Directions:

- Mix honey, gochujang, vegetable oil and salt in a bowl and stir properly. Take out 1 tablespoon of the sauce and set it aside then add Brussels sprout to the bowl and stir until the sprout is mixed properly

- Place the Brussels sprouts into your Air fryer, set heat at 360ºF and cook for 15 minutes; shake the basket halfway into cooking time and set the bowl aside when the timer is off.

- When the timer goes off, increase the temperature to 390ºF and cook for another 5 minutes

- After 5 minute, put sprouts in a bowl and cover with reserved sauce and stir.

Nutrition:

Calories 128

Fat 4g

Carbs 20g

Protein 3g

Conclusion

Thank you for purchasing this book. The book was a result of my sincere endeavor to offer you fantastic air fryer recipes for two. It can help you indulge in healthy eating by not having to bury the desire to enjoy deep-fried foods. I have been creating various air fryer recipes that are easy to cook for a long time, and this cookbook consists of various types of air fry recipes for two.

The Air Fryer Toaster Oven has eight smart programs that give different cooking modes to the users, which are as follow:

Air Fry: using this program, to cook oil-free, crispy food, whether it's coated meat or fries, everything can be fried in its Air fryer basket.

Toast: the temp/time dial used to set the temperature and cooking time can be used to select the bread slices and their brownness when they need to be toasted using the Toast cooking program of the Instant Air Fryer toaster oven.

Bake: it is used to bake cakes, brownies, or bread in a quick time.

Broil: the broiler's settings provide direct top-down heat to crisp meat, melt cheese, and caramelizes the vegetables and fruits. It has the default highest temperature, which is 450 degrees F.

Roast: this cooking program is suitable for roasting meats and vegetables.

Slow Cooker: The Slow Cook program lets you adjust greater cooking time and lowest temperatures based on the requirements.

Reheat: using this mode, the users can warm up leftover food without overcooking the food.

All the recipes are quick and suit healthy living. The delicious air fryer recipes in this book are categorized by breakfast, lunch, dinner, appetizers, seafood, side dishes, snacks and desserts. Tried and tested recipes were used in this book to make sure that the foods taste good exactly the way how you cook with a conventional appliance for deep frying. You will get the crispness, the fried aroma, the browning, taste, and what not.

My collection of air fryer recipes would be the biggest inspiration for you to switch to a healthy version of fried foods. This book will be a detailed guide on how to cook some of your favorite meals without using oil that will not just be healthy but also packed with texture and rich flavor.

You can forget about the menace of oil, which create havoc to your body and one of the main culprits to make people obese. I have taken special care to include recipes that are simple, tasty and easy to prepare are for people with a busy schedule and life. I wish you all a happy, healthy living and a new style of cooking!

Though, people who wish to have a balanced personal and office life, sometimes find it impossible to spend quality time with family by cooking a good healthy meal. An air fryer and a cookbook with recipes can help you make it a thing of the past. The cookbook, loaded with a rich and satisfying collection of recipes, will let you enjoy warm accolades from everyone who tastes your air fryer food.

While an air fryer seems like a specialized and expensive kitchen appliance, it is not the one that would sit on your kitchen countertop forever. In addition to cooking healthy fried food, you can also grill, roast, bake, stir fry and steam in this delightful appliance. I'm sure you would end up using it every day to eat healthily.

If you don't have an air fryer, purchase one now or if you already have one, but you rarely use it, check out my simple yet delectable recipe collection to get started. What more could you ask for? Now is the time to change the way you cook. With an air fryer, you can recreate and continue enjoying that deep fried food you loved but may have given up just because it is deep-fried in excess oil.